T0381304

AuthorHouse™
1663 Liberty Drive
Bloomington, IN 47403
www.authorhouse.com
Phone: 1 (800) 839-8640

Published by AuthorHouse 05/02/2018

ISBN: 978-1-5462-3709-9 (sc)
978-1-5462-3708-2 (e)

Library of Congress Control Number: 2018904610

Print information available on the last page.

Any people depicted in stock imagery provided by Getty Images are models,
and such images are being used for illustrative purposes only.
Certain stock imagery © Getty Images.

This book is printed on acid-free paper.

A DESIGN OF HIS OWN

MIKE EATON AND VIRGINIA FORTNER

Table of Contents

I Plunging In

When Marianne Eaton asked me to write her husband Michael's story, I knew little of his extensive history with the surf. He was the attractive, mustachioed gentleman in shorts and aloha shirt beside his wife in St. Augustine's pew most Sundays. His 80th birthday was announced one warm December Sunday morning, along with two other octogenarian residents of North Kohala on Hawaii's Big Island. I suspected that his wife's mind was busy preparing for a huge backyard party for neighbors, friends, and family to celebrate that milestone. I usually tried to sit near him and the visiting priest during brunch so I could catch Mike's latest funny story. On January 18, 2015, his name was among the Kapaa'u, Hawaii congregation's prayer concerns. Mike had suffered a massive stroke.

During the next year, I watched him go from being unable to speak and barely able to swallow mashed food to the still-attractive fellow scratching one-word notes and telling surfing stories from memory. Occasional tears surfaced, a post-stroke symptom of emotions, as he shared stories from a wheelchair in his sunroom. Whales navigated the visible channel between Big Island of Hawaii and Maui beyond our North Kohala view as Mike launched immediately into memories of surfing days.

"In California in 1947, we had a 'Swim a Mile' Club. Tom Blake, the lifeguard, was my hero. He gave me an award the day I swam five miles. I was twelve. That was at Palos Verdes' Local Plunge."

Marianne interjected, "Michael swam a mile again yesterday, using just his right side!"

Mike sidetracked long enough to tell me his strong right arm is Ramon, and his left one is named "Claudia—CLAWdia, 'get it?" because it was slowly becoming less like the claw it resembled after his stroke.

He returned his focus to surfing memories: "Tom Blake was the first to put a fin on a surfboard. In the beginning, most surfers used 'kooks'. If a kook box, with its round bottom, got unbalanced, you pearl dived--went one way and the board went flying the other. You just had to go to the bottom and wait for those 70 pounds to come down somewhere you weren't. Later Pacific Homes made balsa redwood boards, but only the good guys had 'em."

We had a quarter-dozen more weekly meetings, chock-full of Mike stories, and I received a call from his wife, Marianne. "Mike had a heart attack."

Doctors conferred as Marianne and caregivers attended Mike in sleepy North Kohala and Waimea on the tropical northern tip of the Big Island. I waited several weeks, wondering if we would be able to complete what we'd started. The day we began talking again about his life, I took lemon bars to share. He chose to plunge immediately into remembrances of surfing, hot-rodding, gliding, and sailing. Marianne asked him, "Aren't you going to eat one of these, Mike? Virginia made them." He quipped, "Of course. I've been eatin' (Eaton) all my life." and reached for the treat with his useful right hand.

Our pattern of meetings resumed. I would read his words and story resulting from our last time together, he or Marianne would clarify dates, names' spellings, or sequences of events and we would begin a new topic. Sometimes, I held a surfing journal or photograph of restored cars so Mike's right side could take in the picture. He focused in and brought the story to visual life. Mike's cranked-up hospital bed-- surrounded by walls of pictures featuring him, an Eaton surfboard covered with autographs, and bookshelves of magazines and books flagged with stories and interviews featuring Mike--usually had one of two ever-present Jack Russell terriers lounging on his lap or above his shoulders. The TV, if on, often featured car races, which he could only see when his right eye triggered his brain to focus on the screen. When he noticed the "Eaton" emblem in the shape of a fish on my tee shirt, he recollected, "People in California saw that emblem on my van running all over when I delivered boards there."

Mike had written sketchy notes for our first meeting; after that, he simply asked, "What's the day's topic?" and jumped right into well-told stories. His memory was uncannily sharp, his wit even sharper, and the twinkle in his eye increasingly present as he spun tales of his adventurous life.

Weeks turned into months, and I arrived one August day to see an even-wider smile on Mike's face. He had walked again at Waimea's Therapy Center. He told it like the dialogue of his first solo glide in California. I heard:

"The therapist: 'Today, you're going to walk from here to that bookcase over there.'

Mike: 'By myself? No walker?'

Therapist: 'Solo, my boy.'

Mike: 'Are you sure I'm ready?'

Therapist: 'You're ready.'"

Marianne told me later that three therapists, a wheelchair, and the walker stayed close by as Mike made small steps and pushed through fatigue across the room.

He assured me "It's still baby steps, but it's progress!"

I asked him what would have happened if he hadn't made it. He grinned. "They'd pick me up, I guess. But I tried to do everything I could to prevent it." It was a milestone, and Mike was feeling proud.

That was also the day I learned that, around 2010, he was treated with radioactive seeds implanted to cure prostate cancer. "It wasn't aggressive and I was a good candidate—a fortunate chain of events," he explained.

Until his stroke, he had frequently done Kamehameha Park's Relay for Life around the local baseball field, honoring other cancer survivors. He and Marianne walked the nearby Upolu airport road regularly in the past. Now, a caregiver pushed his wheelchair down, but not as far as the historic *Mo'okini Heiau* toward the ocean below the Eaton home.

Mike explained a bit about *Mo'okini Heiau*, a stone's throw away from where we sat in his sunroom. "It's one of Big Island's oldest and most sacred heiaus, built in 480 A.D. King Kamehameha I's birthplace is nearby. People tuned into the spirit world say it was used for human sacrifice. You can get chills down there," Mike warned me. I increasingly got an understanding of why Mike often returned to Hawaii since first coming in 1968 and why he and Marianne chose their home's particular spot.

More often now, he thought of a book, picture, or trophy he wanted to show me and would have his good leg swung off the bed's edge as he said, "Let me show you….it's just in the other room…" In my mind's eye, I was already calling 911, knowing I could not pick him up if he left the bed and went down. An often-present caregiver, Marianne, and I had to use our persuasive powers for him to let us get the item. His brain was ready to go while his body was inching toward mobility. I was grateful there were plenty of distractions outside the sunroom windows to direct attention back to accomplishments to ask about—such as building the raised beds for herbs, pineapples, flowers, and vegetables Marianne planted in their yard.

Mike was equally at home introducing me to Manila Gorilla, a stuffed white animal above his pillowed shoulders when his dog Buddy wasn't in that spot. Manilla Gorilla was a gift from his younger sister Anny. He reminded me, "We called her 'A'."

Mike's 'Angels,' girls from his Hawaiian *ohana* (family) who cared for him in the hospital, made sure the gorilla was on his pillow after his stroke. Mike said, "Manila Gorilla stayed with me the whole time." That meant Anny's gift went with him when he flew to Honolulu for care also. I later learned that Mike had given Anny a fuzzy bear when she went through some rough times and that bear had also been with her ever since. Those brother-sister bonds seemed strong, bound by tangible, stuffed toys.

Asking about pictures on his wall, I learned that, until the stroke, he was a docent for 130-year-old St. Augustine's historic tour during their annual Fall Bazaar. "I like to keep busy," he said." I didn't miss the annual Canoe Club luau at Kawaihae until last year." He chuckled about paddling with the Kawaihae Canoe Club when founder, Uncle Manny, put Mike "in with some bikini-clad girls in great shape and they just about killed me!"

He'd barely had strength to enjoy his and Marianne's favorite sushi restaurant's fare when the paddle was over. When asked about how many paddles he'd refinished here in Hawaii, he said, "Probably hundreds. They get dinged up real easy."

We talked of early January 2015, when Mike was Volunteer of the Year at Kohala Resource Center, just down the road in Hawi. He confided, "The nicest thing about the Resource Center was I got to read their books between visitors. I loved to read. Now, reading's a chore. It's a real loss." I expected tears to well up, but Mike took it in stride.

He recalled his volunteer days in yet-another story. "If anybody came from out of town to the Visitor's Center, I sent 'em to places with history. I'd read up on 'who built what when' and hiked to quite a few of 'em myself. It was fun. A woman donated books on ancient Hawaiians that couldn't be checked out, so I'd read when I wasn't busy and add to my stories from there." He answered tourists' questions and, directed them to waterfalls, King Kamehameha's statue, heiaus, or Pololu Lookout. "Just drive to the end of the road, but be sure you have good brakes!" would launch him into telling how the first Hawaiian king grew up in those deep valleys.

That brought Hawaiian storyteller-musician Kindy Sproat to Mike's mind. "Pololu valley was also home to Kindy, who sang at Carnegie Hall. He told stories of Kohala's early days. I always tried to point newcomers to Kindy's book."

I thought how Kindy didn't have the corner on a storyteller's stories. Mike's had me hooked on his life's stories from our first meeting.

Backyard View

Michael with Manila Gorilla

Mike Surfing in Baja

Photo of St. Augustine by Rev. Bruce DeGooyer, Vicar

II Early Years

A few years after his birth, 12-30-1934, Michael Eaton's mother told him, "Halloween would've been more appropriate than a late Christmas present for your birthday, Mike."

When Mike was almost seven, Pearl Harbor was bombed. He recalled whole camps of Army soldiers marching up and down the street. He dug a foxhole and played war with a pop gun as P38s flew down the coast on training runs. He knew his Uncle Bill flew one in the Pacific. That probably launched Mike's interest in airplanes. He also remembered playing with kids of Japanese farmers who leased good ground and grew vegetables around their houses. When the war came, they gathered the vegetables and disappeared. Mike didn't understand where his playmates had gone.

In his words, "I was a rowdy kid. 'Got tossed out of third grade. Father Ford caught us drinking the communion wine, and that was the end of my altar-boying. Palos Verdes Country Club had a cocktail hour, so we kids would be sent off to find something to do. One time, we saw a pretty cat outside, 'Oh, look at kitty!' My younger brother and both sisters spotted it and ran over to it. I hung back, maybe because I knew what it was. Anyway, I was the incidental recipient of the skunk's benevolence. All four of us walked in, heading for the dining room, and the people at the cocktail party said, "Get those kids out of here!" We all had gotten a squirt. Mother had to scrub us down with tomato juice when we got home."

Mike's sister, Anny, recalled a neighbor, Oliver Field, who liked Mike so much he gave him a cap gun with the admonition, "Never point it at anyone!" The next time when Oliver drove by, there was Mike, taking aim. Oliver stopped the car and took away the cap gun."

Anny also told of a chemistry set that arrived one Christmas. "There was an explosion that burned younger sister Drusilla's leg. Mother cared for the *owie*, took away the chemistry set, and that was the end of that."

Jared, born five years after Mike and now living just up the street in Hawi, saw his mom as the caretaker who tried to please all four kids. He remembered Emma, their housekeeper, as a constant in their household, a help for Mother's responsibilities where raising children was considered women's work. He recalled, "Mother's comments were simply 'I don't like it…' to let them know that she didn't approve. Daddy's comments were more along the line of 'Don't bother me with your problems. Solve them yourself."

It was a time for kids to develop independence. Group therapy was frowned upon, as was anything "touchy-feely". Public shows of emotion were considered crass and improper. It was a time when communication stuck more to facts and avoided feelings. Jared summed up their growing-up days. "Mother did her best. She was a loving person. As far as I know, none of us had any problems with the law."

Mike's memory kicked in, his thoughts drifting toward the ocean reaching from his present HI life to his early CA coast years: "Around age ten, I'd walk the dirt road a mile to the Bluff Cove Lookout to watch surfers. They were the Hell's Angels of that time. My mom was neutral about the whole thing, but Daddy was a little disturbed. He didn't put clamps on me, but he'd say, 'Get a real job, kid!'"

Mike's family remembered rattlesnake skins complete with rattles, hanging on strings from the 2 x 4s in their garage. His penchant for collecting rattles continued well into Mike's teens. Jared, their friend Phil, and Mike hung out a lot in the Eaton garage--a greasy trio. Mike's room often had car parts in it too.

Both Mike and Anny had vivid memories of family meals. Mike reported that "Her kids were the most important thing in Mother's life. Our European background included wine at dinner and fed us well: salads and stews, lots of canned foods and eggs."

Anny, also living just up the HI mountain from Jared, recalled that their mother set a lovely table. When Grandmother Jaccard was present at Sunday dinner, there was a decided French influence on formal dining. Before the days of TV, the Eaton family sat each night at dinner. That gave their parents an opportunity to teach manners. Daddy, especially, conditioned the family toward table behavior.

All heard "Are you going to a fire?" when anyone hurried eating. Mike sometimes got his knuckles rapped with Daddy's knife for things like talking with his mouth full. When Mike and Anny, picky eaters, would refuse or turn up their noses at a dish, Daddy would finally say, "Oh well, all the more for the rest of us."

Mike mimicked Daddy, "Lift your food to your mouth. Don't put your mouth down to the food. Is your arm glued to the table?"

He chuckled at the secret ingredient--orange juice--in Mike's mom's pancake batter. "We four kids would grab a plate and keep her running from the stove to the table. The family joke was that she couldn't make a waffle to save her life. They always stuck."

Mike paused to grin, then kept reminiscing. "We drank lots of milk. It came in glass bottles. The kids scooped out the cream with their fingers, much to Mother's dismay. When delivery got to twelve quarts every-other-day, the milkman said he'd give us a cow."

Once, the half-dozen Eaton family members took the train from the Los Angeles station to the Cliff House, famous for fish. Mother and Daddy enjoyed lobster while Mike insisted on a tuna salad sandwich. They stayed at the Mark Hopkins hotel in the heart of San Francisco. Both Mike and Anny remember that young Jary got a wooden cable car and pushed it on the stair rail from the bottom floor to the top, making appropriate car sounds all the way.

There were also weekly trips to Hermosa Beach to see Grandmother Jaccard. She had married Swiss Jules Jaccard after Mike's grandfather, George Francis Eaton, died when his father, Francis "Red" Eaton, was six years old. Her second husband, Jules, had been a non-conformist with a beat-up fedora and a New York car dealership. He probably influenced his step-son, Mike's father, toward interest in hot rods and sports cars. Mike recalls his dad regaling his family with napkin tricks and adventures from around the world. That may have given the Eaton kids their penchant for adventure and travel.

Sister Anny tells this story: "After attending mass in Redondo Beach, Mother took us to Dopey's in Hermosa Beach for doughnuts." She recalled that "Mike ate tons of doughnuts. He seemed 'way older when he sat at the far end of the counter, which he also did when we went to the drug store for hamburgers. After doughnuts, we picked up Grandma and drove back to Palos Verdes Estates. She stayed with us for the day. Daddy drove her back to her little apartment at Hermosa Beach after dinner."

Anny filled in a few earlier facts: "Grandma Alice and her husband, Jules Jaccard, moved to Luasanne, Switzerland, where Jules had spent most of his young life. Daddy and Mother went to Switzerland and were married there. They spent a couple of years in Juan les Pins in the south of France. After Jules died, it was time for Grandma, Daddy, and Mother to return to the USA. Michael was born December 30, 1934."

The ever-present Pacific washed back into Mike's memory. "Anny, Drusilla, and we boys were water bugs. Mother would drop us off at the local plunge and pick us up at a certain time. We didn't get in much trouble."

"Mother had her hands full. I was oldest, then two girls and a brother in five years. We lived in a Spanish style house built in the 1920s. You could see ocean sunsets from certain portions of the house."

At the time Mike's dad bought the Palos Verdes house, 1935, it was country living. "The Beach Boys lived nearby; my brother knew them, but I didn't. The neighborhood had maybe 900 people on the entire peninsula." Mike knew that, if he got in mischief, his mom would know about it before he got home. Everybody knew everyone else.

It was pre-television days in their household, but Mike recalled enjoying Captain Marvel comics, along with the radio waves bringing Bing Crosby's and Gene Autry's music, the Green Hornet's serial adventures, and "The Shadow". Mike broke into a wicked laugh with "Who knows what evil lurks in the heart of man?....ha, Ha, HA!"

Some of the same pictures from his early years hang in Mike's present Hawaii house: Homer Winslow's print of *Eight Bells* elicits a description of Mike's great grandfather as a ship captain and his daddy as a naval submarine officer. He pointed out how Winslow's painting depicted a noon shot by a guy on deck with sextant in hand to navigate. Mike reminded me, "No GPS then!"

"Chris Arens' <u>Twilight in the City of Angels</u> parallels the era I grew up in. There was Malaga Cove Public School, St. John Bosco's Boarding School, and graduation from St. James School at Redondo Beach. There, Brother Albert was a good teacher and mentor who helped me grow up a little bit. We used to play soccer and catch river polliwogs in the L A River."

"I remember playing 'Red Rover, Come on Over' at school. Super Mom drove us there and a few other places. My daddy, born 1894, I think—early enough that he went to Buffalo Bill's Wild West Show. Daddy had been class president at Peddie, back east in New Jersey. They sent me there for high school. I never did quite fill his shoes, but (Mike paused, wiping a tear) I think he'd have been proud."

Another childhood memory involving their daddy came via Jared. "Mike really liked 'Cool Water…Keep a movin', Dan…Don't you listen to him, Dan' on records we'd play. Daddy's friend, Ralph, would come over for martinis and they'd talk about his movie connections. We can still tear up, hearing 'Cool Water'."

Mike's father, a popular guy, seemed to know everybody. Mike recalled a stay with Lowell Thomas, national reporter, while "the men talked of stuff over my head, and I twiddled my thumbs."

Daddy and Uncle Bill formed Peninsula Game Company. They had worked on a card table game with a sports theme, and the 1949 trip was made to pitch it to Parker Games Company back east. Electronic games had just gotten a start, and Parker wasn't interested. Mike soon dismissed that disappointment. "Salem, Massachusetts was a great place. I was in Seventh Heaven! After two hours in the Peabody Museum, Daddy had to drag me out by the collar."

On the Route 66 drive home, "Ferdinand the Bull"--their 1930 Model A roadster with a V8 engine--opened up and became a gun-metal gray blur. An Olds 88, a hot car then, screeched by them and someone yelled, "What the heck was in that Model A?"

A storm came outside Oklahoma City where the lightning and thunder never seemed to quit. They survived the car spinning around at one point. "That trip was an important father-son bonding time." Mike grinned. "I got the liking for cars—sort of a genetic defect—from my daddy."

Anny clarified the linkage further--Mike's grandmother married a Swiss car dealer. He was her first husband. Her second, Mike's step-grandfather, had other interests; however, Mike somehow emerged with a strong liking for automobiles.

Jared recalls growing up. "I was Mike's grease monkey. Mike'd say, 'Give me a 3/8 socket wrench,' and off I'd go to get it. We went on short surf trips too. At the Lighthouse, I'd stand on the sidewalk and listen to the jazz, but Mike was old enough to go in. There was the West Coast Jazz club with Bob Cooper on sax, the All Star Band… Those were fun times."

Growing up wasn't all socializing, cars, and surfboards. Mike was also into hiking and backpacking. "I wouldn't mind doing it again when I get my faculties back together," he said, adjusting the Velcro cast holding his left foot straight. His mind wandered back to favorite trails in King's Canyon and another story: "It was a beautiful area. I had a girlfriend at the time who took her top off to hike. We met a bunch of giggling Boy Scouts, but it didn't faze her." Mike's laugh left the rest of the story to imagination.

He digressed to further explain King's Canyon. "I loved hiking the snowy mountains. That was where Walt Disney planned to make a ski resort. There was a big protest, and Walt opted out on that. Unfortunately, it was an ideal place for a ski resort—close to L A and San Francisco with lots of snow. One year, it snowed so much there were bears on the roofs trying to get into cabins. David Bradley would've designed Disney's rides; I built a boat for him once. He kept a lion in his back yard. It was tame, but you didn't push too far. Anybody interested in breaking into that house was in for a big surprise!"

He went back to the topic of school, "Richie Clark and I grew up in the same town with Malaga Cove teachers who lived next door to each other, the Reeds and Wrights—reads and writes, get it?" He fixed his right eye on me to see if I understood the pun, then continued. "I talked Richie into going to Peddie with me."

"I hadn't made the most of the California schools, and, when we got there, I heard 'Do you want to flunk or be put back?' I said, 'Let's give it a go,' but I definitely wasn't a threat to the folks on the dean's list. Geometry and General Science were my best subjects; Latin was probably my worse 'Amo…amas… I can still conjugate verbs.'"

About that time, Mike bought a hot rod from a fellow he knew in Hermosa. He drove it across the country on Route 66 to Peddie in New Jersey. Since cars were not allowed, a girl friend's grandfather kept the car at Decker's Dairy Barn with the trucks in Heights Town, NJ.

One car Mike drove with Richie to school and back to California was the Yellow Peril. It was written up in the Philadelphia Inquirer. "Once it ended up in a Ford agency show room. It had nickel plated rockets, no top, no fenders. At the end of the 1950 school year, we two 16-year-olds--Richie and me--drove it on Route 66 (on the way) to CA. We'd stop at some sleazy motel with holey sheets and wallpaper peeling off the walls-- not much money then. The Yellow Peril burned up Thunder Road many times."

"Once along the windy Blue Ridge mountains in Tennessee, it was so wet and cold that Richie said, 'I can't feel my fingers!' A guy let us stay for free, and Richie was first in the hot shower. Lightning hit the water main with a loud bang. Richie flew out of the shower and under the covers."

"Another time, it rained so hard in New Mexico that we had an inch of water on the floor of the car. In good weather, you could see down thirty miles of straight roads on that trip. When weather was wet, it was another story."

When asked about surfing in those formative years, Mike remembered, "Around age six or seven, I sat on Bluff Cove. There were no movies or magazines to distract us then. We listened to Riverwalk Jazz on the radio though. At The Plunge, bordered by Haggerty's Estate, Tom Blake—the guy who first put a fin on a surf board-- loaned me a board and said, 'Go paddle.' That started it. My uncle built a hollow plywood board before he went to war, and he gave it to us kids in the late 40's when he came home."

Mike transported his heavy wooden board to Palos Verdes Cove using an army stretcher customized with rear-mounted wagon wheels. He longed for something lighter, but he had to exercise some patience.

"Bob Simmons was quite a craftsman. His board was a technical masterpiece. I was around 14 and didn't have $70 for it. Daddy was assistant golf pro, managing a golf club where I worked summers. Daddy was good, but I didn't get very decent at golf. Anyway, he helped me buy a

Simmons that I used until I got one hand-shaped by Velzy around 1950. The Simmons board was a real piece of work, but well worth the cost and wait. Good balsa wood was hard to find, so Simmons made boards with Styrofoam core, balsa rails, and a plywood deck and bottom. Redwood boards weighed about 100 pounds. Kookboxes weighed around 60, until they leaked. My Simmons weighed 45. I thought, 'It'll not get better than this.'"

"That first board had a skag like a water ski. There were no leashes then; they went into play in the 1950s in Santa Cruz. Before that, if you fell off, you went on the rocks. The leashes were made of surgical tubing and, if you let go, they'd 'ping back'. Jack O'Neil lost an eye because of surgical tubing. Jack had gotten a wet suit free in the 40's and later gave it to me. I used it, then passed it on to my brother, Jared, and friend Phil for $5. With that wet suit, once I'd hit the water at Steamer Lane, I thought heaven had arrived."

Mike heard a rumor that Greg Noll, who showed high school shows, was making a movie. It was called *Slippery When Wet*. There were few enough surfers in San Francisco to count on your fingers when Mike went to see Noll's movie. He also read Jacques Cousteau's Silent World and joined a dive club. By 1957, when Mike was discharged, he was dismayed by the increased number of surfers. The movie *Gidget* had kicked off the surfing craze.

"Movie extras and blue-collar workers who wanted nothing to do with that time's ritzy club celebrities made up the Malibu Yacht Club. We learned other ocean skills on Malibu Outriggers. The Yacht Club formed from a mixture of clubs just east of the pier."

Mike made a boat in California and brought it to Hawaii. He translated its name, Zangano de la Playa, as "Beach Bum". That brought him full circle to swimming with dolphins and paddling with the Kawaihae Canoe Club in North Kohala's retirement, still keeping busy.

1949 St James Basketball Team, Mike 2nd from left top

1950 Peddy School Baseball Team, Mike 2ⁿᵈ from left top

Mike and His Mother 1983

Zangano de La Playa & Trailer

Zangano de la Playa

III First Wave

Life changed for the Eaton family mix when 18-year-old Mike and Nancy got married. Jared felt mad because, in his words, "It took my brother away". Mike remembers the humor, like each April Fool's Day when Nancy would tell him she was pregnant. He still laughs at himself. "I fell for it every year!"

The arrival of Debby, Mark, and Drake meant hard work, more mouths to feed, and increased responsibility. His family lived where Mike worked shaping a few boards for Jack O'Neil, on boatyards, or close enough to ride his bike to work. There wasn't much chance to catch waves, like when he was single and living at home. In contrast, the rest of his family moved to a newly-built house at Lunada Bay, a district in Palos Verdes, around 1954.

Mike also moved along his LA beginnings by joining the Coast Guard in 1953. His first job after basic training boot camp was as a telephone operator. It didn't go over too well when he unplugged the base commander one day. During the Korean War, Mike was put on a new 90' patrol boat to the San Francisco harbor entrance to escort ships that had touched Communist ports.

"On to Aviation Machinist School at Elizabeth City, NC. It was tough—80% studied hard and dropped out." Mike figured his experience with engines helped. He got the opportunity for initial training at Alameda. After graduation, he asked to be stationed at San Francisco's National Airport.

While in San Francisco, Mike went to Underwater Swimmer's School and became friends with other skin divers there. He'd met his mentor, Jack O'Neil, at a surfer movie. Before Jack and the Body Glove brothers designed and built wet suits, surfers wore old sweaters and anything else they could think of to stay warm. They wanted sunny days. After wet suits, they could surf anytime. Bob Meistrell became the number one dive instructor in LA county about the same time as he and his twin, Bill, developed wet suits. The Body Glove name came from the Dive and Surf shop owned by their parents. Mike dove with all of them and recognized an "I did it first" competition among his friends. Jack was first to get excited about surf leashes. They used rubber tubing, like big rubber bands with a suction cup attached. That pinged back and cost Jack an eye.

Jack asked, "Mike, 'Know how to shape?" Mike had made a board or two, so he answered, "Sure!" They made a few in Jack's garage. Mike recalls, "Nothing to look at now—no power tools, balsa boards."

In addition, during the 50s and early 60s, Mike was raising a family. His first house, costing $13,000, had three bedrooms in Hermosa Beach. Upon learning that the first child was on the way, Mike's mother said, "Thank God. Now I'll have some grandchildren. No one else in the family seems interested in giving me any." Three children came through the thirteen-year marriage to Nancy, who had attended middle school with his sister Anny.

Brother Jared told of Mike's riding a bicycle to work. "Mike and Nancy lived a couple of years in a gatehouse at Portuguese Bend on Abalone Cove. It was a beautiful situation for Mike. He worked for his rent."

"Mike also had crew accommodations for his family on Terminal Island at San Pedro's Boat Yard—Multi-Hull City. We did sail and work at Multi-Hull City where we realized the vicissitudes of the economy—feast or famine. He'd had a taste of shaping with Jack O'Neil earlier. Also, Bing Copeland was in Hermosa, not far from our boatyard. Mike would bike to work, make steady money, and have time off for surfing and jaunts. Then, about that time, his marriage started to fall apart."

Jared further explained, "Earlier, around 1952, Harry Benedict, emissary of Frank Vanderlip—president of New York City Bank and later NY City Corps—thought they'd get rich. They developed the Tuscan motif for Palos Verdes' development. It was well-planned."

Mike added his story. "Frank Vanderlip was a friend of the family, active in the community. His family occupied the hill that stuck out of the water. It was from a Spanish Land Grant or something, and Frank was going to build a Hearst Castle. My brother lived there at one time. I got permission to live in the gatehouse at Abalone Cove with Nancy and our two kids."

Jared took it from there. "But the crash came. The investor in our little shop with four employees making Nugget Trimarans shipped the work to England where there were craftsmen. He made his money later investing in aviation radios."

"Mike had lost the goose that laid the golden egg. And he had to figure out how to make a living. Mike left his Marineland job and tried to make boats. He refused to collect unemployment, built a few outriggers, but his kids were hungry sometimes."

Mike said, "Nancy wasn't an ocean person, but she didn't discourage me. Ours were good kids, but full of mischief. Deborah—Debby—came first, then Mark, and finally Drake." He spoke with pride of Debby, being much like her aunt, Anny, who took care of his mom after his daddy passed.

He told of Mark's 40-year-ownership of a bike shop, and Drake's middle name after Grandpa Hardy's 1846 ship's papers framed in Mike's Hawaii home. "Francis Drake Hardy Eaton is quite a moniker for a little kid who got up hungry one morning and pulled out an onion and took a bite like he would an apple." Mike laughed. "He won't eat onions to this day."

Another family story is about a babysitter who saw young Drake fall two stories from their window ledge. Mike and Nancy came home from a movie to see her "as white as a sheet of paper" and called the doctor. "The doctor said he didn't hit his head; he bounced. He could've landed on the grape-stake fence!"

When Mike worked at Marineland, Debby the Dolphin was his special charge. Owners Frank and Boots collected porpoises and whales and brought Mike the beautiful dolphin that he trained. "Life magazine carried us working with trainer, Cliff Tucker, and animals like Bubbles, the whale. They had special cameras and shot roll after roll. If you take enough pictures, you're bound to get a good one."

It was 1960, the year his daddy died, when he arrived at Marineland in his 1934 Ford primer. If the family came to see Debby do flips and take food, they drove the Corvair station wagon. He used those wheels to take Mark, and later Drake, skin diving.

Mike also trained a 13' Boston whale, Bubbles, at Marineland. "It was a lot of fun for a few years, but it had a limited future. Marineland served its purpose. It was popular, paid off in a short time, and is now dismantled."

"People used to ask me, 'What does your wife think when you come home smelling like a fish?" recalled Mike, without revealing how he answered that question about Marineland days or their marriage. He simply continued, "Debby got the idea first that things weren't right at home. The divorce was complete in 1965."

Mike said that he saw the children every once in a while and sent money. "They knew I loved 'em and vice versa." He is a grandfather eight times and a great-grandfather nine times. "Mark's youngest's son, Michael, father of the most recent addition to Mike's great-grandchildren, gave the boy the initials K.J.E. Mike punned, "We'll see if he's 'cagey' this year."

He trained his good eye on a collage of family and friends with ever-smiling Mike on the wall and pointed with his good hand. "That's at my granddaughter's wedding—Ana Rubio's in Ventura. The good-looking guy is Martin, my grandson." We wheeled Mike in to gather around the computer and view pictures of a surprise visit from Patrick Dempsey. He was filming Grey's Anatomy while Marianne waited as a girlfriend had surgery at Hollywood Kaiser, just down the street from the TV studio. Mike appeared next in pictures around Kohala, collecting signatures on a doll that great-granddaughter, Carly, sent to "go different places—like farmer's market —so she could make a report for school."

Mike looked up to the signed surf board above his trophy shelves. Memories returned to his working days. "In the late 60s and early 70s, I was making twenty boards-a-day, doing piece work, and doing well for a while. I'd put my head down and do ten-hours-a-day. I also went surfing every chance I got. Bing's team guaranteed two-week delivery. That was unheard of then! That's when I worked on the Bonzer. Campbell Brothers had the impressive idea in an 8 mm movie. I got favorable feedback and shaped over 15,000 Bonzer boards over the years."

He recalled, "We made boards for Rolf Aurness, a quiet guy who beat an Australian for the World Surfing Championship. We also made boards for his father, James Arness, who became Matt Dillon in Gunsmoke."

More rich and famous surfers surfaced as Mike remembered shaping surfboards. "We also made Charles Spreckles' boards. He was Clark Gable's stepson. Bunkers was his given name—part of Spreckles Sugar." The early cane operation's museum operates now on Maui.

Mike's ever-present grin widened with the next memory. "During those times, I made more money than I could spend, but I was willing to give it a try!"

On 9/11, 2013, on their thirtieth wedding anniversary, they renewed their vows at St. Columba's Episcopal Church in Pa'auilo, on the other side of the Big Island. They wanted to get married in church this time. The wedding in 1983 took place on a 151' schooner with 150 people attending.

Then came 9/11 of 2016. I promised Marianne I'd be at St. Augustine's for the blessing on their anniversary. She pushed Mike's wheelchair to the front and they stood, arms around each other, holding hands with another couple celebrating an anniversary. Mike wore shoes, sox, and sported what looked like a new haircut and mustache trim. The priest blessed them. That scene contrasted with the remembrance of an earlier 9/11, infamous in America's history.

After church, they left to prepare for another eventful time—a weekend at the Waikaloa Hilton down the Kona coast. It would be their first time since the stroke to get away by themselves. Mike was hoping to swim in a "place I've visited often, but never stayed there before." Marianne gathered the four-legged cane, the pills, the wheelchair, and—I suspected Manila Gorilla went into the vehicle with their luggage.

30th Renewal of Vows

Flat Carly with Marianne

Flat Carly with Michael at Hawi Farmer's Market

IV Setting Sails

When asked about his interest in boats and sailing, Mike suggested we watch The African Queen featuring Bogie as sea captain. That led him to recall a boyhood memory. "My California friend Matt's grandfather owned a big schooner that was in LA Harbor where we used to camp out on the weekends. We'd walk around the docks in the evening, looking at all the boats. One summer, Humphrey Bogart's head popped up from a boat. He called, 'Hey kids, 'you want a Coke?'" It was a celebrity moment to savor and another move toward building boats later.

An article in The Surfer's Journal names Mike Eaton as the clean-cut bronzed surfer-sailor on a Seaman-designed boat with a main sail of 192 square feet. He remembers that "those boats were featured in *The Endless Summer* and around the California coast until Hobie Alter built a 14-foot catamaran with a centerboard-free design. Hobie Cats rose in popularity during the 70s and replaced Malibu Outrigger designs."

Jared, five years younger than brother Mike, gave his interpretation of early boat-building days. "Mike was a good mentor for me when our father was absent, often. Mike had a natural talent that showed up in Polyhull Boats, our business at Hermosa Beach. I had dropped out of UCLA and was having fun sailing. Because of that interest, I joined Mike to help with the accounting. We're both hands-on people, acculturated to business by our dad."

Their small shop made Malibu Outriggers. Mike cut his chops, did the woodworking, and built a nice Class C racing trimaran. He designed it as an extension of a 19-foot one he'd built earlier. Jared mused, "Joe Dobler designed and drew up the plans. We got to know South Bay sailing people around Santa Monica in the '50s. One of the most significant might've been Warren Seamon, whose son later became a shaper and small boat builder—catamarans. Others like Rudy Choy and Alfred Kumalai's *Aikane* broke the trans-Pacific record; those sailing enthusiasts still charter boats."

After Mike left Marineland as a porpoise and whale trainer, he began making 18' Malibu outriggers, after his first one, a 12-footer. "These were poly-hull boats, aesthetically pleasing, but very wet. When the bow punched through a wave, there was lots of spray. Once on a sail from San Pedro to Santa Monica, low in the water there was no wind, and I walked up and tipped my sister Anny in up to her chin. She scrambled back in the boat—with nothing worse than her cigarettes getting wet; but solid water hit the rest of a long race, and she was miserable. We approached the finish line with the boat shuddering. She was shaking the whole boat! Her boyfriend brought her coffee and she shook it all over too. Annie didn't offer to crew for some years after that."

"I went on to build a 24' Malibu that was nice and dry. I usually sold boats by word of mouth. I usually sold 'em before I started 'em." Another thought surfaced to balance Mike's memory equation. "I made a windjammer, 'good in the cold winters there in California. I sold it for $10 at a garage sale and have been kicking myself ever since. It cost about $80. I could've used it here."

"We sailed to Catalina a lot—from our house at Abalone Cove there. I raced Malibus a fair amount, 'won our share of races and helped the sale of boats. The idea was to get a girl in a bikini to distract the competition. One of my boats won class championship in a series of races, but I wasn't crew for that one."

Mike formed the Polyhull Boat Company after building the Malibu Outriggers. Later, Nova Tech Electronics bought the company and hired him to run it. "Electronics was booming, and boats became a pain, so the company decided we were no longer an asset and therefore they didn't need us anymore. 'Beat it, kids; go find somewhere else to work.'" Mike remembered.

"About this time, people noticed that I was a pretty good sailor. A guy I knew, Don, built a boat by himself in San Diego—a 45' schooner named Styx. Boats look big on land. On water, they shrink. Don and a girl sailed along Vietnam and the Philippines where they came across a refugee boat sinking with 40 survivors on it. Don was set up for four people, but they were conscientious and gave aid. The girl left, and he wrote me from Singapore. 'I'll pay your way if you sail the boat back." It was 1978, I had decided to start my surf business and had time."

"I landed in Japan, went in and got my passport stamped, flew to Singapore, where I blindly stumbled around. I knew the boat was on Pongo Point, so I got a taxi there. In low tide, we propped it up in mud. Over the next six weeks, we scrubbed and painted the bottom, did lots of work, and I got to know the boat. During that time, there was a nice supermarket and little restaurant where I ate a lot of Indian curry. I'd always wanted to go to the Raffles Hotel and have a Singapore Sling like Humphrey Bogart, so I did."

"At high tide, the boat floated with an auxiliary engine. Earlier, Don had tried to get permission to bring the refugees ashore, but nobody would let them. Thailand finally had let them come ashore, but they had confiscated all but one or two of Don's rifles. Out on the open sea, we got wind and headed up toward Thailand on the South China Sea. Here came a rough, raggedy boat. We heard, 'Yankee!' and Don disappeared down the hatch."

"A rifle came flying up. Don yelled, 'Hold that up so they'll know you are armed!' He knew another sailor's wife had been raped along there. I was thinking, 'What have I gotten myself into?' We took off as fast as that fishing boat could go. They pulled in somewhere and left us—Philippines or Thailand? Don went ashore in a dingy and got back our confiscated rifles."

"Off we went. We sailed up alongside Japan and didn't touch land after we arrived at latitude 40 and got favorable winds to California. Out in the open sea, we came across a pinnacle—Job's wife—sticking up. No more land for eighty days. At one point in the northern Pacific, we were as far from land as we could get and still be on the planet."

They tried to catch water in the sails and took showers when it rained. Nature fortunately provided. "In a squall, we get a good fresh-water rinse and set out buckets to catch rain. It wasn't the best sleep—three hours on watch, three hours off. Sometimes, we towed a hang rope along behind to swim beside the boat for a free ride. We didn't fish—if you caught one, there was no way to refrigerate it. You'd look and drool when a big tuna swam under the boat. I don't know if I could've landed one. I'm not much of a fisherman."

"I grew up on PB&J—strawberry or raspberry jelly, so peanut butter was a staple on the boat, along with canned tuna. I'm not a cook and am kind of a picky eater to boot."

"On the way back came the roughest part of the whole trip. Still three days out of San Francisco, a knockdown—too much sail up—tipped us over so far that the sails were in the water. It was a violent maneuver. I watched everything around me washing away and kept thinking, 'Don't let go now!'"

"Don yelled, 'Mike! Mike!' I didn't answer--in shock, I guess. He thought I got washed overboard. Nothing broke, fortunately."

"Don's dream was to sell Styx for a 60-footer when he got back to California. I told him, 'No, on that 60-footer, there are just lifelines to hang on to. That one's a man-overboard boat!' Sure enough, it did happen later near the Philippines. His three-man crew heard the sails flap and never found him or knew what happened."

Mike paused at that memory, then returned to boat-building stories. "My little boat company got a reputation. I got interested in some Arthur Piver-designed Trimarans. They came and asked me if I'd sell, bought it, and hired me to run it. I ended up building 24 Trimarans. They were called Nuggets--seaworthy, not racing boats, Piver was known and criticized; he'd do designs on butcher paper, mostly for home-builders he assumed knew what they were doing. Some came out less than originally expected. From Mill Valley, a fighter pilot during the war, Piver managed to sail one 30' across the Atlantic."

Jared remembered Piver this way. "Arthur Piver designed trimarans of plywood. It was a simplistic design by a backyard builder—they could be found all over then. Mike became interested in marketing it. He improved the boxy design, improvised hinged cross-arms so you could trailer it. Mike had an instinctive design sense."

Another Piver memory brought a sly smile from Mike. "When asked what he thought of the mini-skirt, Piver said, 'The End is in sight!' I liked the guy."

The smile faded, and Mike turned serious. "Piver wanted to single-hand across the Atlantic in a 24' Nugget. He disappeared between San Francisco and Mexico. I think a big freighter ran over him. They never even found any wood from the boat. He was a good sailor, but when a freighter comes up fast at night and doesn't see you—end of Piver story. 'Except in our bathroom there's a picture of a Piver-design, *Ariga*, built for a San Diego dentist. He sailed it to Honolulu with his son as crew."

"Here's a red-faced story," continued Sailor Mike. "I was working Terminal Island, San Pedro, in L A Harbor, and had to go under the Henry Ford bridge to get to ocean and deliver a boat to an owner. I was motoring along about five knots when I figured out the Henry Ford was a drawbridge. Luckily, there was little or no damage. The mast went back up the next day."

"I also remember running alongside a grey whale. I could've stepped off on his back. I was going about ten knots, and we were about the same length."

"I built a day sailor. The Triad-designed Wil-O-Wah raced a lot. It was a good, comfortable boat where I got to have a crew and not torture them. I sold it to my brother. I also designed a 20' catamaran to World Class A classifications. Its first race, we headed for the harbor with great anticipation and found no rudders—they were detachable. Late to start, we capsized, and never made it. We did sail in with the finishers, so bummed out we drank Mexican coffee until we were bleary-eyed. I wanted to sleep, but the coffee gave me the whirlies."

"I designed and sold a bunch of plans--24 or more. One I built for Neil Harvey, Australian cricketeer. The El Gringo won L A's Class A Championship. His sons are also very good sailors. I built the whole boat plus trailer for $600. You couldn't do that now. I loaned the master plans to somebody, never got them back. It makes you heartsick. I can't tell how many hours of labor went into those."

That statement was about as close as Mike came to voicing regrets over the months we met to sketch out his life.

Mike on one of his sailboats

V Fast Wheels

It was a rainy day in Hawi Town's island paradise as I parked my scratched Ford Fusion in the Eaton driveway and walked past Marianne's scooter. Her black Honda 150 wore a silver cover to avoid damage from salty sea mist in the air. Inside, Mike's hospital bed was cranked into sitting position, and he was eager to reminisce. I moved to his right side, the best place for seeing and hearing. His right eye focused on a snapshot of him, shirtless at age 18 in 1952, posing with his shiny Yellow Peril on Thunder Road. That led into stories of his love affair with cars. "I guess we start when motorcycles entered the picture," he began, and we were off and running.

"My very first was a paperboy bike with a belt drive. I'd take it apart just for fun. Next was an English Ariel, and I got fancier bikes as the years progressed. They were mostly dirt bikes. I had a black and red Spanish Bultaco that I really liked. I rode it to work and in the desert. It was simple, probably a collector's item now. I had a few Hondas and road bikes. Once, I took Polly Beale (Ridgeway), my gliding friend, on the back to Lake Tahoe."

Mike's grandmother's second husband, Mike's step-grandfather, was a Swiss car dealer. Mike figures his daddy (Francis Drake Hardy "Red" Eaton) was the real "car guy with a genetic defect he passed on to me." Mike's first hot rod was a Model A Ford rearranged with a V-8 engine. He arrived in it to get his learner's permit, passed the written exam, and heard the examiner say, "I'm not getting in that thing. Get a real car!" He finished the exam in his daddy's Model A.

"I had innumerable cars; I didn't build any, just kept them running. It was usually solitary, but we did groups sometimes. The races were really fun, like Laguna Seca. I knew a few of the guys; we'd camp and make it a boys' weekend out."

"Once, I had a Wizzer motorbike, a paper boy bike. It's a collector's item now. I reached down for the carburetor and got a spark plug wire. It shocked the hell out of me. I wobbled and crashed. I used to buy used two-cylinder Hondas with air-cooled engines, lower the running gear and the whole affair. I found so many damaged Hondas to swap out engines and running gear to put in my name that I heard 'Mike, you're going to have to get a dealer's license if you keep this up!'"

Around '48 or '49, younger-sister Anny remembers Mike and a friend, Matt Overton, driving far down the Baja in a jeep. Matt's father was ill, but wanted to move to La Paz, so the boys got the adventure of long-distance driving over dirt roads. She supposed Mike flew home after they delivered the jeep. It was a formidable trip for adults in an up-to-date vehicle, but the teens made it successfully—Mike guessed "800 miles over rutted roads". Whether either of the boys had a learner's permit to drive is lost to memory.

In 1950, Mike rebuilt a '27 Model T body on a '32 Ford truck bed frame. "It had a supercharger on it. I drove it on Route 66 (toward Chicago) to the East Coast and back, sold it to a California friend in 1953. He drove it to Florida, also along Route 66 (on the Southern route). He still owns it." Mike recalls, "The car had no fenders, top or hood. Sometimes, when it rained, you'd get about an inch of water on the floor, open the door, and it'd whoosh out. We called it the Yellow Peril."

Marianne brought out a Ford Club trophy that read "9th Annual Ford Picnic, San Diego Regional" awarded to "Best 1932-1940 Ford". Mike indicated a photo on his wall. "That's the Blue Meany, a 1934 Ford five-window coupe. It was midnight blue. Depending on the lighting, the shade looked black in some light.

Mike wasn't through yet; he asked for another photo of a shiny red roadster, beautiful with lots of chrome and a rumble seat. "I used to hang out at Norm Francis' shop in El Cajon, California. One day, I saw chrome parts in the loft there and asked Norm about them. He said he was building a car for a man living in Colorado that couldn't afford to finish the car and they were his. So I gave the owner a call. 'Got it from this guy who went broke, so I paid about 30 cents on the dollar. The 1929 Model A roadster and those parts, wooden dash board, and rumble seat made the centerfold in a 1984 car magazine. It won the Merced Best Pre-40s Award in San Diego County." We found a September 1984 copy of Rod Action, with several color pictures of Mike and details of the Ferrari-red roadster's re-creation in a 12-page article built around the centerfold.

Car memories kept coming back to Mike. "I used to go to rallies, quite a few, I guess. That picture's Ian Thompson's mother in the passenger's seat with me in the fancy roadster. We converted him to a car nut. That red one's a 'cartoon car', not practical. I didn't restore the engine, just detailed it out. Sometimes it's a shame to put a body on the frame. I traded it for two cars—an everyday roadster and a 1940 sedan."

"One day I started looking for surf down the Avenues at Redondo Beach—Avenue A, B, C, etc.—and a car pulled up. I turned around to see a driver with a big cigar. He was driving a 300 SL Mercedes, now a greatly-imitated classic. The Gull Wings opened up, and out stepped Velzy. I didn't expect to see him; he was more of a motorcycle guy. In decent condition, those Mercedes are worth $80,000 to $90,000. If you want to see the 300 SL, watch Jay Leno's Garage. His is worth around $12 million. It might be informative, plus Jay's a character anyway."

"I still love to race. With my Honda, I'd tell it 'Kirkwood,' and the little thing would head for Tahoe. Putt-puttin' along… Porsches would go by and we'd putt-putt on. Pretty soon, they'd notice us again and say, 'How'd this guy get ahead of us?'"

Mike regularly watches "Formula One Indy" car races and "MotoGP" on television. Marianne laughs and says she has endured the sound of car races and motorcycles going around the tracks for 35 years.

"I had a 1970 Honda, around the year Hondas were first made. In the early 70s, in Sun Valley, I found some black ice in the Honda and spent two hours spinning. Those things were like shoeboxes with doughnuts for tires. The frame had everything set on a belly pan; we'd gradually be scooting on its belly in the snow. We really had fun!"

Anny remembers years of greasy teenage guys hanging out in the garage, someone—often Jared--running up to Mike's room for car parts, and hearing a lot of talk about engines as she grew up. Jared recalls growing up, five years younger, as "I was Mike's grease monkey."

For over a year I had noticed the familiar blue Eaton Subaru Baja sitting in the drive each time I came to gather Mike's stories. His wheelchair was increasingly folded in the back, ready for an outing. At summer's beginning, I didn't see it as I entered their plant-filled entry. Mike's voice came booming. "Did you see our new car?"

"No, maybe Marianne took it, since she's gone too. What did you get?"

"A Subaru Outback, same color as the old one. We did some research!" Evidently, they'd decided that a newer version of what they had was the best for them.

He had one further memory for me from cars in California days. "We did drag race a little too, cruised local drive-ins and beaches—wherever the girls were. The drive-ins had those girls on roller skates with burgers." Mike's mind was on cars as a young man, but he'd evidently noticed the opposite sex at the same time.

Mike grew serious for a moment. "Now gliding, on the other hand, is kind of a solitary thing. You land and call home. 'Honey, I'm on highway such-and-such in a field. Bring the trailer.' That's not on most wives' To-Do List."

Marianne's relatives in Mike's Roadster

Mike, Debby, Mark, and 1960 VW Pickup

Teenage Mike

VI Smooth Gliding

Mike began his gliding story in this way. "I was driving my VW near Pear Blossom, CA, in early 1960s. I had noticed the gliders that flew along Palos Verdes cliffs years earlier, before the war. That day, one landed in a field, and I told myself, 'I'm going to do this!'"

He jumped into his Volkswagen and headed for the back of the San Gabriel mountains, where he found the Fixed Base Operation (FBO), an organization using an airport to provide aeronautical services, including flight instruction. Mike told Howie, the instructor, "'I wanna' sign up." He added, "After that, I loved soaring more than I thought I would."

It couldn't have been an easy course. The handouts to download before showing up for a first experience checklists' 78 pages to bring (from forms to weather maps): Homework (computations, drawn wave and ridge lift profiles); Documents (from medical records to pilot certifications plus Aerodynamics like spin vs. spiral dive and Approaches for landings); Cross Country (Assembly/disassembly); Local Procedures (noise abatement rules, call outs) and Equipment (magnetic compass).

Mike remembers the beginning, "I said, 'I want to go flying today!' The instructor got us all strapped in and wiggled the rudder. He had a rear-view mirror so he could see behind. Gliders have one wheel, so they tip over when resting. There's a boy who runs alongside to take the wing up. The pilot releases the tow line. He wiggles the rudder, and that's the signal for 'OK, go!' After the glider gets airborne, the pilot can release it. The boy gathers the lines after the tow plane stops, ready for the next guy. That was the start (of gliding adventures)."

"In 1965, Howie—a great guy and instructor—said, 'Today's the day. You're going solo!'

'Are you sure I'm ready?'

'You're ready. Go!'"

"I had accumulated three hours with an instructor at that time, got a thermal, and went to 14,000'. I saw the channel, Catalina, and Santa Barbara. I couldn't quite see San Diego. It was great! But I had to really work to get down--you get so much uplift and fly away or brake to increase drag and lower or you slip sideways. It's not always smooth before or after a thermal, or a bubble of air. You look for bumps to get lift, feel it, turn into a wing and circle the thermal to spiral up or down. If it weakens, you leave and go look for another. In cross-country soaring, the variometer is the instrument that registers the rate of the aircraft's climb and descent. It's really a sensitive barometer, is what it amounts to. You see a cloud forming and zoom the ship for it."

"Getting down that day required me to make a decision. I couldn't afford to make any mistakes. When I got down, I heard, 'Atta boy! 'Great judgment.' That was worth a lot."

"I actually bought plans to make a glider, but decided I'd fly them, not make them. I did build some interesting things—giant, motorized surfboards-like for Navy Seals to put bombs on the bottom of ships and stuff. And there was 'Dan Gurney', a high-speed gurney that Marianne's clinic could use to speed patients across the street to the hospital. They didn't use it very long."

San Diego was too close to the ocean, and the air too unstable for Mike. He kept soaring from Warner Springs FBO—southwest of Mount San Jacinto, east of Mount Palomar. One day he fancied a damaged plane resting on one wheel and the tip of its wing. It was built in Romania, but he thought he could fix it. He recalled, "I flew that Lark several years; it was high performance by then-current standards, probably not anymore."

"A group of six-or-so of us San Diego Glider Guiders flew out of Brown Field, a pretty primitive airstrip, and figured the Ocotillo Desert would be a good place to go for a decent glide. A Brown Field guy offered to tow us out there. They'd hook up two gliders at the same time, go over the mountains, cut loose and look for updrafts. You could tell where they were far better than in San Diego. We had a good time at Brown Field. Once, here came Captain George Powell, chief of the Pacific Fleet, with his hand out to shake mine."

"I'd caught a thermal over Palm Springs. It was getting dark down below, still light where I was. It was crazy. I couldn't account for why everything was working so well--smooth, just like I had a motor. I tried to make a pattern entry. I think George got them to line up cars with their lights on; otherwise, it would've been like seeing a ghost in the dark. Afterward, we got together telling hangar stories. I still didn't understand why the lift was there that late in the day. The next day, a guy came and towed us to Borderland—it's not on the map—and gliding wasn't any better. Every once in a while, you get a really good day soaring like I'd had."

Mike went into another gliding story. "There was this woman pilot, Polly, who hang-glided into some electrical wires. She got burned real badly, but it didn't kill her enthusiasm. I bought a two-place glider and set her up after she recovered. Now she's an FFA Designee." A 2017 website clip shows Polly Ridgeway, flight test examiner, taking the viewer over the San Jose Valley in her sailplane.

"I took Marianne up once. It wasn't very good conditions. We were circling a mountain. Sometimes that looks scary. She said, 'I want to go down now!' You don't want to scare a person, but you gotta' do what you gotta' do. We went down."

This time, Marianne interjected a correction. "Michael, I only said 'Do we have to fly so close to the rocks?'"

Mike nodded. "Sometimes the wing tips drag alongside of the mountain." They both agreed that they went down after that.

Michael Getting Ready to Fly

VII Second Wave

It was the third May day of Big Island sunshine and 80-degree temperatures as I knocked on the Eaton side door flanked by blooming orchids. The tropical vine had grown at least a foot since I'd last been there. Marianne Eaton, with a new strawberry-blond bob, called off two barking dogs and asked me to wait. "I have to cover Michael up!" She returned, laughing, "He doesn't usually wear clothes these hot days." Mike, with the hospital bed cranked into sitting position, clutched a white gorilla to his bare chest.

I was reminded that Manila Gorilla was younger sister Anny's gift when Mike had his stroke. The back story gave insight into Mike's loyalty, generosity, and family ties, as told by Anny. "I think I was an adolescent until 30," she said. "I was always leaving and coming back. Mike was often there for me with good advice. He and Marianne had only been married a year-and-a-half when I got a divorce. He gave me a teddy bear to see me through. I still have it."

Anny continued. "Mike put his arm around my shoulders and said I could stay with them until I got through it. Can you imagine? They'd only been married a short time. My short-time stay lasted ten years!"

In the Eaton's Hawaii home, Buddy, the Jack Russell terrier, assumed his position on Mike's stretched-out legs. Mike introduced the Jack Russell near the feeding dish, as "Hoover" because he ate like a vacuum cleaner, and "Buddy" because "This is his Buddy."

We then naturally began with the recent turn his health had taken. It was my first time to see him this month since a heart attack. Marianne tried to explain the scare they'd had when his responses slowed and he complained of pain in his chest. He listened with keen eyes, then turned to his life story and earlier health history.

"I've been disgustingly healthy." Mike began. "The stroke happened when I wasn't paying attention to my meds. My doctor left town around Thanksgiving in 2014 and never came back and the office dropped me like a hot potato.'"

Marianne re-entered from directing a care-giver in the kitchen and explained, "I worked in a heart clinic in San Diego. That was where we used Mike as a guinea pig and found he had a bad-looking heart. The cardiologist said his fitness helped his heart stay healthy. The doctors here found atrial fibrillation and put him on blood thinners."

She laughed again. "I took out a 15-year life insurance policy then."

Mike grinned too. "In 2000, they said I'd be dead in ten years. Now it's 2016 and we're both retired here.

Marianne efficiently arranged pillows and straightened Michael's position with the same strength she showed when Mike transported her to San Francisco's Bay to Breakers Run, the third Sunday in May years back. She'd worn an "Eaton Surfboard" logo tee, but there was plenty of nudity at the starting line. One totally nude couple had a baby, also in his birthday suit. Mike "raced for the finish line, but a group of Ethiopians got there first. With 70,000 runners, somehow, I missed her," he said.

He recalled how they met with, of course, another story. "I owned an apartment building in San Diego, and there were three girls who had been my roommates at one time. One worked with Marianne at the Scripps Clinic, where they worked on Nixon. She's done everything from heart caths to radiology—worked hard! I guess it was around Christmas in early 80s when we met at a party. We each were there with someone else, but I liked her smile. She also had a cute fanny."

In 1982, there was a surprise birthday party for Marianne and mention of an unexplained limo ride that brought an exchange of knowing glances. The 2016 conversation took a turn to their last anniversary and Marianne's birthday four days later, when Mike sent his caregiver to pick out an expensive blouse and swimsuit cover-up plus some turtle earrings, ordered a German chocolate cake, and surprised her. He explained how "Boiling water in the kitchen is the only thing I'm good for" as the caregiver washed dishes, sending kitchen sounds from the other end of the house.

Mike was ready to resume the courtship story. "Marianne had broken her leg, so she spent more time away from work with me. I'd go over and sit on her couch with Magic, her cat. He was a great source of entertainment, I'll tell you. He'd pull my magazine out of my hands or go in the kitchen and push the butter dish off the table. You think I like butter? He'd eat the whole thing!"

Marianne's eyes lit up as she told about her Seal Point Siamese, a pre-Mike gift from another boyfriend. "Magic lived to be nineteen." Buddy, definitely Mike's dog and now designated to become the care dog, moved contentedly to the mattress, just above Mike's pillowed shoulders. The story took a detour to tell me that 'Ratatoulli won't be making noise on the roof" now. The rat, named by Marianne, had "gone to another dimension and was no more"—the way things happen in the tropics. I was glad "Bob Barker", Marianne's nickname for noisier Buddy, hadn't tangled with the rat.

Back to their relationship: it picked up momentum when Marianne and Mike hooked up for her to cry on his shoulder about another surfer. Mike asked her to marry him on April 1, 1983. He grinned. "That way, if she said, 'No', I could say 'April Fool'!"

She said yes. The marriage, September 11, was on a 151' schooner, *Invader*, provided by Larry Briggs as a wedding gift. *The Invader* was later outfitted for commercial use by the public. It was a lovely place for one attendant each, guitar and duo musicians, hors d'oeuvres, and cake to celebrate their wedding.

They both recalled the Ocean Beach house that Mike had since 1977, with fondness. "They still have terrific block parties. We were friends with our neighbors." Marianne recounts.

Mike added, "Julie and Craig Klein. Auntie Marianne practically raised their daughter Jenna."

"We camped and surfed at Baja a lot. Phil Becker, who knew Jary—'brother Jared, aka Jughead'-- since babyhood, nicknamed us 'The Bickersons' because we would get snappy with each other on the long drive to Baja. Big Red's tires didn't fit where the trucks made tracks, so it was bumpy, and you had to be on the ball and not drive at night. About 500 miles down the coast, you look for the turnoff—no sign—and go on about an hour off the highway, you take it easy so stuff from the shelves doesn't end up on the floor. That meant arrive in the dark after a two-and-a-half day drive.

Two framed photos show them setting up camp with Big Red, their camper, trying to secure an attached awning in a gale; another serene beach scene shows a roaring fire. Mike said, "Marianne was a great camping partner. She discovered salt water soap. Down there, you get stinky, but you can soap up with it and live relatively human-like. She's a good cook. We ate like we were right at home—fresh fish. We had a lot of fun at Baja. One Thanksgiving, a guy brought a smoker, caught a big halibut—smoked halibut and turkey in the middle of nowhere! Fishing there was outrageously good, but I'm not much of a fisherman. A neighbor and surfing buddy called Smitty came back, holding a halibut by the gills with its tail dragging the ground. He was 5'6" or so, and he'd caught it in the tide pools, just threw out a line. We'd set up and get a storm. You'd hear 'Knock, knock' and look out at all those little domed tents. 'Can we come in?' 'Well, there's not really much room.' If it was bad, we usually brought them in. We were pretty well fixed, especially when we got the VW Westfalia. It was easier than Big Red with a camper on the back.

There were also lots of ski trips—Sun Valley and in California, sometimes with Mike's sister, Anny, Mike told of Marianne's trip after recovering from a broken leg from the prior skiing season. "We were on the way up, and there were five baskets coming down the lift, all with people with broken legs. She didn't let it phase her and went on to ski again."

Marianne's eyes misted a bit. "Michael was a beautiful skier. He usually got down before I did, but if I was at the bottom, I could pick him out. He was so graceful that his speed didn't show."

Mike had the last word. "To be honest, I might be a better skier than a surfer."

When asked about their move to Hawaii, Marianne said, "Tell about the 'V King', V for victor and the design on the V-bottom surfboards. 'Just another nickname Phil gave Michael.'"

Mike added, "They were difficult to make. No one wanted piece work then. I thought I'd make dough doing that, so I did. I put all of it away and, with Marianne's help, paid off the '77 house and factory. I knew they'd be wonderful investments, and they were."

They spent a bit of time visiting Mike's brother and sister-in-law on the Big Island, as well as his sister's family. On their lanai, Anny asked, "Why not move here?"

"Sure, but not if I have to work!" Marianne said.

Their house sold sooner than they thought, and the German Shepherd and cat had to wait on quarantine for three months, so they lived in a friend's basement with a view of San Diego Bay. Mike's brother-in-law worked for Trade Show booth builders, so he got them help to pack the containers. They landed in Kona, expecting an empty Hawi house awaiting their containers. A call came, "Would delivery tomorrow be all right?"

"Everything went 'click-click', even to the big going-away party before they left. It felt like Easy Street."

Mike was happy to retire in Hawaii. "I didn't want to see any more foam. Well…actually I made five boards here. Then I got into outrigger canoe paddling, having fun refinishing paddles. They'd ding up real quick, and I'd enjoy the easy work on them and seeing a quick finished product."

Marianne's days were full too, with galleries and care-giving. She spent time on making lauhala bracelets, orchids, gardening, and refurbishing an ohana on their property for a rental. "She's an excellent cook," Mike interjected. When asked about preparations for her annual Christmas Day Open House, Marianne explained how *pierogis*, her heritage's specialty, involve two days' preparation. "You make a kind of ravioli dough, let it set, roll them out, stuff them, then double the batch. It's time to do it again this year."

There were plenty of visitors from the mainland. One memorable family hike on the trail off the highway at Pu'u 'O'o vent sent us to the computer for pictures. "Six of us piled in—two in the truck bed in the rain. Mark's son, the Eagle Scout, was least prepared and borrowed a light blue woman's raincoat. We got there after three hours and saw, 'Trail Closed' and decided 'Let's hike anyway.' We went through fern forests so thick we couldn't tell which way the sun was from. 'Come on! Don't dilly dally!' We had to get there and back, and it'd been three hours' hike already. Jary took off following markers that were probably farmer's markers. We weren't sure we were on the right track. It started to feel cold enough to take your breath. So we decided we'd have to spend the night under the canopy of two big umbrellas. It was teeth-chattering temperatures! We spooned on the bed we made from palm fronds, three under each umbrella. I was on the edge, so the umbrella poured water on me all night."

Marianne remembered, "Patti knew where we planned to go, so she called the police when we didn't come home by midnight. When we heard helicopters at the break of dawn, we knew they couldn't see us through the forest canopy. We heard 'Stay where you are' and quit running and tried to make a clearing."

Mike took over. "Two hours later, here was the helicopter with a basket dangling. I thought 'Here it comes!' when I saw the Ranger vehicle. 'Oh brother! We'll get fined.'"

"Michael was the oldest and the coldest, so we sent him up first," Marianne interjected.

Mike took the story another step. "I thought, 'Oh dear! A police escort! There was a Hilo cop walking toward me. He stuck out his hand. He was one of my customers. We never did get a bill for the rescue."

The stroke surprised them both.

"Marianne can't be given enough credit for caring for me this past year. My stroke was a total surprise. I fell out of bed, and Marianne said, 'You had a stroke.' I said, 'No. Other people have strokes.' She called 911, then she and sister-in-law Patti drove to the hospital. Doctor Jackson didn't think I was going to make it. And those little Filipino girls—I call them my angels—took care of me, always smiling, and they were good at it."

Mike's eyes misted, and Marianne interjected. "The nurses helped sneak the dogs in after visiting hours one evening. When we finally brought Michael home, the dogs were in the drive, waiting."

"And that was the start of Marianne's Health Care Service!"

Asked if home care was difficult to arrange 12 hours each day, Marianne started to answer, "I'd been doing home health care here a few days a week… And neighbors like Buddy Bohn and Mike Stevenson helped me get Michael out to the pool and ocean about a year after the stroke."

Mike added, "Buddy Bohn, retired lifeguard captain at Malibu, lives here. He essentially carried me down the Kawaihae boat ramp for 'Up, Up and Away' dips. We've got pictures to prove it!"

Mike turned back to focus on his wife. "Marianne knows everyone. Just the other day, somebody at Farmer's Market asked her, 'Are you famous?'"

Marianne answered, "No, but my husband may be!"

The tides continued to rise and fall as Eaton caregivers came and went with Marianne's bulletin board chronicling the changes in meds and routines for Mike's progress. Nine of us gathered for Thanksgiving in Eaton's sun room with Jared, Phil, and Mike exchanging memories of boats, boards, and cars. After the traditional meal, Marianne, Jared, and Patty took plates to Anny and husband, Dick, just a few blocks away. Two days later, word came of Dick's death. At the Veteran's Cemetery near Kona, I learned about the extraordinary life of Mike's brother-in-law, who began most mornings with, "I have an idea….." I found myself beside Mike's wheelchair as mourners touched the cremation box for one last blessing. Mike looked up at me and said, "It's the beginning of the end of the old guard."

Another evening, I found myself beside Mike's wheelchair at 100-year-old Bamboo Restaurant for *pupus* and Happy Hour music that gave background for chitchat with friends. Marianne and Mike had been to an Italian restaurant down the coast a few days before, and we heard that "the spaghetti and meatballs were to die for!" I was glad to see them getting out more, although I knew it was quite a production to transport everything after getting ready, expecially since caregivers' time had dwindled with time since the stroke. Mike, happy to be out and about, trotted out a few tales of early days for a CA transplant at our table. Suddenly, he turned to me with a serious face.

"I've decided when I sign this book, I know what I'm gonna' write. *"Don't give up!"*

Camping in Baja 1985

Camping in Westfalia

Hike in the Fern Forest

Michael in Chairlift

Michael in Kawaihae Harbor with Brother

Michael Swimming with Buddy and Jared

Mike and Marianne's Hawaii Sport, 2010

Snow Skiing

VIII Old Friends

When asked about influential friends in his remarkable life, Mike began with Tom Blake, who contributed to board design, wave-riding technique, competition, photography, and surfing literature. Blake brought a Polynesian curiosity into a 20th century lifestyle, actually defeating Duke Kanahamoku in a 220-yard sprint. Around age 9, quiet Tom Blake saw a surfing movie clip. After wiping out, he waited three years to try again. Mike may have admired Blake's restrained attitude, along with his bigger-than-life style that made him a legend. Waterman pioneer Blake shuttled between Hawaii and California often, fascinated by the early Hawaiian surfboards during his visits to Bernice Pauahi Bishop Museum. He studied the longer boards reserved for royalty to the shorter *alaia* style favored by Duke Kanahamoku. In 1929, Blake applied for the first U.S. patent on a hollow surfboard. In 1936, he set a run record estimated at 4,500-feet near Waikiki.

Mike recalled, "Tom Blake was a hermit, in a way; he lived on a boat in the Ala Wai channel in Honolulu, later moved to a Malibu ranch. He was the first guy to surf at Malibu Point, one of the few catching waves at that time. Blake paddled Catalina-to-the-mainland several times. I'd see him out by himself. It was impressive. He used to go tandem with girls—boards were too heavy for even a strong girl then. After we began to make hollow boards, they were much lighter."

"Tom Blake was my hero. As a 12-year-old, I'd fooled around in the ocean with no purpose. He gave me direction, encouraged us to exercise. He was fit himself. He lifeguarded at Palos Verdes pool, where I learned to swim. I saw pictures of him surfing when I hung out at the local soda fountain. I guess you'd say he helped me grow up more. I probably saw him in National Geographic around 1935. Anyway, I got exposed to a seminal figure in surfing history, a prototype of modern-day surfers. He spent some time in Hawaii; you can find it in the Bishop Museum."

Mike thought next of Dale Velzy, "Velzy comes into the picture because of his surf shop-- Under the Pier, Manhattan Beach. Velzy was the first to sell balsa boards to specifications. He put ads on tee shirts. No cars yet, so we were early friends and just hung around."

Velzy was a bigger-than-life figure, credited with being the first commercial shaper. He brought the first tees into an advertising medium, had the first surf shop, and was a good surfer himself. His Pig board was a surfing game-changer, probably the reason he's remembered as the Henry Ford of Surfing. Mike recalled, "I looked up to him, and I wasn't the only one. He was popular, and for every true story you heard there were a hundred more you couldn't hear. Marianne reminded Mike, "Velzy had a handlebar mustache like you." Mike shrugged. "As I recall, Phil Becker and I grew one for fun around 1968. I kind of liked it, so it stuck."

Dale Velzy fills three columns in <u>The Encyclopedia of Surfing.</u> Sometimes credited as the first surfer to hang ten; with surfboards, Velzy's popular, balsa-constructed Pig model—dropping a board's wide point toward the tail—changed the sport. He was the king of surf retail in mid-to-late 50s. *The Endless Summer* had one wave—"Velzyland"—named for him, as well as a movie, *Big Wednesday,* based on his life. Mike brought this "chairman of the board" to further life.

Mike recalled, "Velzy was into shooting. He was a 'Marlborough mannish' cowboy who'd worked on a ranch. His wife, Frannie, and he both did leather work—chaps and stuff. They'd load their own cartridges for target shooting. They were also into bow hunting. Velzy would roll in the dirt and change his human scent. He was successful enough at bows and arrows. After *The Endless Summer,* he sponsored the making of surfing movies. That movie was well done—and well received."

"We shared an interest in motorcycles and cars. I gave him money for a modified '27 Model T and traded it back to him. He'd bought it from the wife of a guy who had been killed and Velzy didn't care so much about its hot engine and race motor. Velzy wanted the workmanship on it. It was the only car I had when I was first in the Coast Guard. My wife was pregnant and couldn't fit behind the wheel. It was a sad day when I had to let it go."

Mike continued pouring out stories. "Hap Jacobs grew up in the same town and was about my age. He made me a board, better than I got from Velzy. He ended in a shop on Pacific Coast

Highway—442 PCH—named after a model of a board he made. There was also a surf team 442, who were involved in *Endless Summer.*"

Later, I had a Ford diesel van and got paid for delivery to buddies. It was a good deal for me. They got a good deal too and were relatively certain I'd get their boards there undamaged. Hap rode with me sometimes. I spent my time going up and down the coast delivering boards to proper surf shops, but it was really an excuse to go surfing."

"Hap was a gentleman and an excellent shaper. He and Velzy were as different as night and day and got along like two peas in a pod. Velzy-Jacobs Surfboards--they were the perfect combo for a time. Typically, boards with his diamond logo were sold out from under Hap. Somebody would come in and say, 'Velzy, I need a 9'8". Velzy would hold the tape in such a way that it measured 9'8". Or guys would come in expecting a nice, light board. Velzy would always carry it out for them after they bought it. Hap said, 'I just made a board and it was gone!'"

"We also did some modeling. Hap stood out with his good looks. N. E. Wear of San Francisco asked us to model in Santa Cruz County, along with Pat Farley, an interesting local character. He had long blond hair, in the style of the time, and was the guy they wanted. His brother, Francis, was a champion kickboxer. Pat wrote Surfing to Saigon, 'came out of the Vietnam War with a chest full of medals. The experience included free clothes."

"Hap took good care of himself, was proud of his El Camino, and was as easily recognized as was his specialized boat for sword fishing. That fish is lucrative when you can get one. His son still sword fishes. Hap's store set the precedent for future shops. It was clean and organized, like retail shops; his boards were popular. I appreciated his reliability."

"Bing Copeland was another reliable human being. I worked for him around 1965, and he was the best boss you could imagine. He was one of the pioneers of surfing. After he closed up shop at Hermosa Beach and moved to Sun Valley, Idaho, I stayed with them winters in the mid-70s. Bing didn't really like to ski, but he and his partner there at Beacons Franchise did extremely well. Vacationers came for tennis, fishing, and backpacking—Idaho's a big percentage National Forest—they'd build summer houses and rent them to skiers in the winters while they went down to Baja to swim. Now, if you go to his website, you see he started all over, later, with surfboards."

"Dan Bendickson was another guy I worked with. I worked hard. Becker and Dan would look up in the rafters and say, 'Time to go!' and I'd have to look everywhere to find my stuff. I'd lined up my tools, and they'd move 'em. If I stopped to look for something, it'd cost money. But I took it in stride as a prank." As recently as 2008, fans were blogging about hanging Bing boards shaped by Dan Bendickson on their walls.

Bob Simmons introduced fiberglass into boardmaking. He was bright, smart, intense, and intelligent. Resin and fiberglass experiments came out of the navy. "Essentially, Simmons ushered in a new era by fiberglassing balsa boards. It was more practical than varnishing. A big deal." Mike recalls, "Bob had a misshapen arm that made him paddle funny. He made wider boards. He was killed at Windansea. My guess is a board hit him and knocked him out."

"Grubby Clark provided foam to make boards. He wasn't that interested in grooming and his clothes were sometimes compromised. He had a mighty big operation in San Clemente, and the EPA was giving him a bad time. He tried his best to comply, but it was a continual battle. Finally, he closed. We thought it was the end of surfboard making, but others came along to fill the need. If you called and said, 'I need 9'6" specialty stringer or a set of three stringers, you'd get the blank in a matter of days. Gordon Clark had trucks to deliver, and he developed specialized tools for making the foam. He later took it into the making of flies for fly fishing. Harold Walker made pretty good urethane foam in competition with Gordon Clark, who ruled the foam business. In fact, Clark wouldn't sell to you if you bought Walker. Clark could do that because he had a good product with reliable delivery. You'd see foam blanks tied all over like cartoon trucks on the highway."

"Steve Pezman, editor of a surfing magazine, could both surf and write. We used to go down in Mexico where you could get a room for $1.20, catch a surf break around San Blas, and ride it for a mile. When it works right, you have to use a car to get back to your starting place. Pezman came there with a friend, the editor of another surf magazine, expecting to take surf photos. I was teaching two girls from New York. There wasn't much surf that day, barely enough to get them started."

"I knew who Pezman was then, at San Blas. He's a big guy, six-foot plus and loves to eat. I've made him more than a couple of boards over the 30 years I've known him. Once, I made a real pretty one, took it in my pickup to his magazine, and I slipped as I got it out. It made a gash in the bottom. We both laughed about it, and I made him another one. Not much else you could do. You might call Pezman a roving editor; he later started <u>The Surfer's Journal</u>, more pure, with less advertisement; I guess you'd say he was true to the sport. Up to the present day, I'd say he knows more about surfing than anyone ever thought. His services are much in demand."

"Another person I admired was George Powell, Adjunct General of the Pacific Fleet. I knew he was flying gliders on the north shore of Oahu, Dillingham Field—the WWII airport. He roared around Dillingham for several days. Actually, with no food and no sleep, that's dangerous. They later discontinued that endurance record. As far as I know, there were no accidents though. His 126 Glider was named Snowflake. I went to Ewa Beach one morning, and there was George surfing his Hobie 16 Cat. That surprised me no end. I never surfed with him, but he'd say 'Let's climb such and such a mountain'. That was never done either, but that's ok. He's still flying at past 80, lives in Bonita with his beautiful wife, Suzie."

"The Santa Barbara group came down to San Clemente to try waves another place. San Clemente group would try out Santa Barbara waves. Some crew members got more territorial than others. Renny Yater was guru of the Santa Barbara crew. He was a good friend and associate—a kind of mutual admiration thing. Yater Surfboards developed a following, and his son now makes boards."

Another surfer came to mind. "Dennis Choate was a surfer and board builder from Seal Beach, next to Long Beach, where he had his business. He had a boat-building company, making racing 50-70-foot sailboats and was an extra good sailor. I used to borrow a boat from him and escort the Catalina race. He was a kind of stand-by support. Dennis moved around, went to Peru one time and learned the language. It helped him in surfboard-making there and in California."

Leroy Grannis was an accomplished surfer and photographer in the 60s. His book, <u>Grannis</u>, earned him the New York Times title of the Godfather of Surf Photography. While we looked at Grannis' book, Mike stated, "He was well liked by everyone. He photographed lots of Southern California surfers, especially at Hermosa Beach.""

"I used to deliver August surfboards, Stewart, Copeland, Harbor, G & S, and my own boards. Robert August used me for deliveries. I'd pick up boards at the factory that were sold to the shop, charge the shop, and offered a valuable service for those fragile boards. I had my van and trailer specially set up to deliver them without any damage."

Anny's take on Mike's work as a shaper had to do with memories of Mike's shop. "Mike's shop often had a group of men in it, talking of aerodynamics and things beyond my capability to understand. Someone would say, 'Hey, what are you makin' now, Eaton?' Becker would say 'Ya gotta start sellin' things like shirts and stuff!' Mike would break in, 'They get a shirt when they buy a board. They're on my team then.'"

"Mike's surf shop was a special place. People went there just to hang out. In later years, it was like 'going to see Grandpa'," Anny continued.

Names and memories kept flooding back for Mike to share about others. "Bill Stewart was a talented board-maker, a good surfer himself. He translated his artistic talent into surfboards, where he was also good at graphics on the boards. Mike Hynson, one of the *Endless Summer* surf rebels and a member of Windansea Club, had the Hynson Red Fin with shaper-adapted down rails that brought new shape at the edge of the board."

"Ole Olsen was another old-timer from the early days of surfing. He was a popular guy around Huntington Beach, now on Maui and still making surfboards. Mike admitted, "I was pleased to be in that."

The memories of friends kept coming. "Another key player and good friend was Gary Bond. He worked for me at least ten years. He was an Indianapolis Race Car crew chief. Gary was able to do any job that was required. He helped with a hot wire system, a way to cut Styrofoam and shape boards much easier. He was the first to coat my boards with fiberglass and painted them for me. Folks sometimes took us for brothers."

"Carl Ekstrom was an extra-talented friend, a tool maker. If you wanted to produce something, he could make a mock-up. He was in the La Jolla area, the Windansea Club. I remember one of the funny jobs he had was shaping falsies. He said, 'And I'm getting paid for this?' He also did a device to hold a person's head so doctors could work on the brain. His mock-ups were the exact thing to go from, rather than a drawing. You could write a whole book about him."

"Dick Metz worked for Hobie, ran his shop from the early days in the San Clemente area. It was more of a 'hi' relationship for me. Hobie Alter was a good surfer and great idea guy. He put a center stringer in foam. A lot of the stuff he did was ahead of his time. Once he surfed the wake of a boat from Catalina to, I think, Laguna Beach. I'd seen it done in Galveston--guys sit on the edge of the channel and surf in on the wake of big ships. Hobie's Hawk, a radio-controlled glider, was successful and quite pretty. When Hobie sold his Hobie Cat and got out of the surfboard business, he got into motorized catamarans. He took the big one—60', I think—up to Puget Sound. Hobie deserved induction into the Sailing Hall of Fame. It's a very elite group, 'way over my head. We're talking famous, bigtime."

"Probably the first hard-working shaper who would put his head down and shape significant quantities was Terry Martin. He and Velzy came into Bing's shop where I was working. Dan winked at me and said, 'Shape as fast as you can.' So we really went to work, shaping fast and accurately. It surprised the heck out of Terry. Velzy felt the boards, yelled at Bing, 'You're paying these guys too much money!' We didn't have to reshape any of 'em either."

"That reminds me that Tommy Curtis, TC, was a good surfer who worked for Bing and me. We met in the water surfing Sunset Cliffs, San Diego, and became pretty good friends. If you felt lost, he'd make it happen. We kept up, and he did color work, had a shop of his own after a while."

"Donald Takayama, a Hawaiian born little guy, was also a well-liked character I surfed with. Velzy gave him a job. He started his own boards at one point. Bruce Jones was also a friend and surf-buddy, a good shaper. I liked Bruce a lot—he was honest, ran a nice shop. He was a 'no-BS' kind of guy. He was looking forward to surfing Hawaii in the early 70s and did so, off and on. That was a fun time for 'research and development' between California and Hawaii. We'd shape orders for Bing, then say, 'I'm going to Hawaii.' 'All right' was the answer. Several big name surfers got work almost immediately there. I remember once when Bruce went to Hawaii, rented a car, and somebody stole everything he had in it."

"Dick Brewer, another Hawaiian shaper, was considered 'The Man' by many surfers, maybe held in highest regard, on a pedestal. What makes him 'the best'? That's a question that'll never be answered. The perfect surfboard never existed and never will exist. Different waves require different boards. You'll not get one that does everything. Brewer's refinements did a lot to bring the shortboard revolution into focus."

"Dave Sweet tried to mold surfboards. He had limited success; the surfing community generally turned their noses up because 'molded, not custom-shaped' was the attitude then. It's taken a long time to accept. They're doing it now. I didn't know him personally."

"Rich Harbour was an early pioneer of surfboard manufacturing in the Seal Beach area. He's still going too. Rich was one of the first to have machines to cut down labor on getting the basics done. He ran a retail store, developed a following that made his boards quite popular from Santa Anna to Newport Beach."

"A bigtime surfboard manufacturer, along with Bing, was Larry Gordon, co-founder of Gordon and Smith Boards. He was a religious guy who used to call us heathens. The office people were OK because they went to church. We got along fine; I did what I said I'd do, and he respected that."

"Phil Becker grew up across the canyon from us. My mom heard a baby crying, and went to find Phil, born just a few days apart from my brother Jared. As kids, we'd get around the water with inner tubes until Uncle Bill built a kook box. It was old, obsolete, and used to get water in it. You'd have to stand it on end to get the water out—glug, glug. If the water went to the front in a wave, you'd pearl dive. We were into motorcycles together too. Phil had kinky hair that was easy to spot then. Now, he's gotten streamlined—not much hair. He used to draw caricatures with a band around the head like a monk's on paper napkins. There was a high school art project where he carved a pair of hands. That's difficult to do. The teacher said that wasn't Phil's work. It was so good and so accurate, it was like a piece of fine art. They didn't think a kid could do it, so his dad had to verify it. The hands hung from the mirror in his woody. As shapers, Phil and I probably were the only ones who continued longboards through the 70s. He must hold the record for shaping the most boards of anyone—thousands of 'em. Phil bought real estate in Hermosa Beach and has a house right up the hill here in Hawaii. He first designed and built a North Shore Oahu house. It's beautiful, but crowded over there, so we kept saying, 'Come on over here to the Big Island.' He rides a bicycle here like my brother does."

"I knew Rick Stoner pretty well and surfed with him. He lifeguarded with Bing, did Coast Guard in Hawaii, and came back to Hermosa Beach. Rick started making Bing and Rick boards, then got out of the lifeguard business and went full on with boards. They also went to New Zealand and were the first to shape surfboards on beaches there. He eventually went back to lifeguarding and earned high rank in that organization. In his business, Rick was the first to export boards to Peru. Rick died young. His son, Jeff Stoner, won the Catalina race and is well thought of for his racing paddle boards. They have a well-thought-out logo."

Mike's forehead wrinkled. "I'm afraid I'll leave out some. There were so many friends and influences: Buffalo, Hawaiian old-school King of the Makaha Classic every year on his surfboards. It's magic. Hoppy Swartz was one of the original surf club members. He was called the Father of Surfing in the '30s and organized a judging system for contests in the '60s. He and I first sat on Palo Verdes cliffs and saw maneuvers that led to that system. Hoppy was well built, a classic surfer."

"George Oberlin was another interesting guy whose family is involved with the political structure of San Francisco. I knew him through the shop and as one of San Francisco's good surfers. There's powerful surf there. He liked my boards, and we became friends."

Asked how many boards he'd made Oberlin, Mike said, "Probably dozens." Talk of boards brought yet another longtime friend to mind. "Jim Carter, my paddling partner at Mission Bay, has been a good friend ever since San Diego days. Some friendly boat yard put hulls and pontoons up on their roof. I asked, 'What're you gonna do with that stuff?' The answer was 'It goes to the dump.' I said, 'I'm the dump!' And that stuff sat, probably fifteen years, in front of my shop. Jim would come by and say, 'What're you gonna do with that stuff?' I'd tell him 'I'm gonna build a boat.' That happened several times."

"Jim'd come by again and urge me to live up to my word. I didn't have any money for a good motor. He said, 'Don't worry about it.' He helped me get a decent motor, paid for it, and said, 'Put your money where your mouth is.' Jim's been a good friend ever since. Jim was an ocean swimmer too. He did some distances and helped me with training for the Catalina Race. Mostly, I guess he put his money where I could live up to my word."

I had to ask for more information about the Catalina Classic Paddle Board Race. The internet lists Mike Eaton as one of the well-known participants in 1994, 1995, 1997, and 2005 races. Paddlers use only their hands to propel through 32 miles of swells, currents and wind conditions at dawn, leaving Catalina the weekend before Labor Day. Mike appeared almost as proud of its having first been won by Tom Blake in 1932 as he was of Marianne and 15 others having joined him in 1998 for the Hennessey's Cup Fourteen Mile Race. Marianne reminded him that, in 2005, he was the oldest finisher in the Over-70 category entries. "Yeah," said Mike. "As far as I know, that record still stands."

2002 Eaton Show Room

'89 Ford Diesel Delivery Van

2002 Eaton Show Room

2002 Eaton Show Room Bulletin Board

Escort for 1994 Catalina Race

Mike in Coast Guard Unifom on his 1927 Model T

Mike Paddling Out on his Board

IX Shaping Up

I was saying goodbye at the end of a session, hearing stories about surfing and shaping friends, when Mike grew intensely thoughtful. He'd been thinking about more than just the chapter we'd worked for an hour. He told me, "This book isn't about promotion of surf boards. It's the story of a boy who grew up in the golden age of surfing. He couldn't weigh the gold, but he could feel it. It was the age before the commercialization and crowds, before the hordes arrived. The drug era followed in 68-70s. It was pervasive in the community then. I feel fortunate to have escaped--not innocent, but wiser."

"During the longboard-to-short era, I started shorter 6', twin-fin boards. Then guys began making them shorter—5'6". Those were bad-mouthed as 'herky-jerky', not smooth. The era of surfing had matured enough that guys brought their sons to surf. The older guys are usually out of shape, not young or experienced enough to do a short board, with its square tail end. So there was a resurgence, called Modern Longboards. I was into that heavily. It's always easier to buy longer boards than to wipe out or get younger."

"The way I see it, there's a welling up of old guys to the top. They cascade down and are supplanted by new guys who fill the gaps. The Founding Fathers envisioned civilian legislators who would come out of civilian life, serve, and return to their former lives. I support term limits. No one has a monopoly on good ideas."

"I was a 'Gear Head' or a 'Greaser' growing up. Surfers were anti-establishment," Mike said they wore swim trunks under their jeans and went barefoot to school, whenever there was no surf. The uniform of the day was white tees, often with a pack of cigarettes in a rolled-up sleeve. Mike, however, emphasized, "I never had a desire to smoke."

Mike's attention turned to his high school years back east. His daddy graduated at Peddie in 1914, and "Lo and behold, I went there, just like he said his son would sometime do. It was not without great sacrifice on my parent's part."

Mike's brother, Jared remembers generosity and sacrifice on Mike's part too. "I lived with Mike while apprenticing woodworking and accounting with his business. I learned a lot of good things up there."

Anny tells her story of Mike's caring for family. She recalls wondering what she would do next after a divorce. Mike put an arm around her and offered for her to stay with him and Marianne, married less than two years, until she got things sorted out. "And I stayed ten years!" She laughed, with a trace of a tear in her eye.

With Mike, the decisions and adventure is on a more objective level. He tells it this way. "Experience as a diver made me aware of things the average surfer doesn't confront. Southern California had pretty benign waters, so the most dangerous thing was probably your attitude. I did have a couple of times when I thought 'Oh boy, that was a heck of a wipeout. In the Santa Cruz cliff area, there's a point—Steamer Lane—where it was best to get in the water by jumping off the cliff. It can paralyze your diaphragm. You gasp, grab the board, and get out of the way before the next wave. Countless times, I had good waves there, but the cold was an omnipresence in Santa Cruz. I learned to be very choosy about weather and held out for times when the sun was warm."

"I remember one surfing rescue I had to do. A kid wiped out and was floundering in white water. He was frightened, 'Going into the break! Going into the break!' I heard him yelling, 'No, not again!' But I managed to take us both in. Then he saw his buddies and the shoreline and said, 'I'm OK from here on' and paddled in. I let him do it."

That humility and generosity of spirit did not spread to laxity in Mike's desire for excellent quality in the products he sold. Anny told me, "When he was building boats, the makers wanted the hulls made in Hong Kong. 'Then I don't want my name on it,' said Mike, and he changed the way he made it."

Jared recalled that, when Nova Tech was sent to England, Mike was out of a job. "But he did not collect unemployment." Jared said, emphatically.

Asked if he had some words of wisdom about getting along with people, Mike answered, "A smile goes a mighty long way. No one likes to be around bummers. Around eighth grade, they called me 'Smiley.' That nickname died a slow death. I used to go to the Luau and Longboard Invitational benefitting the Moore's UCSC Cancer Center. They invited us so-called legends. One local, Mystic George, used to say, 'I like to see you because you're always smiling.' I think I've always been pretty much that way."

"I've made a lot of decisions. One might be the move from Santa Monica to San Diego; I've never regretted that. I've regretted a few, not many. I don't look back. I look ahead."

What advice did Mike have for people starting a business? "Do your homework first. Market it for what you're intending to do. Put your head down and go for it. Work hard." He added an afterthought. "More often than not, you'll find out your employees are making more than you do."

Anny's eyes lit up as she described Mike's workshop atmosphere, from intense green walls and bright lights to illuminate every nuance of the foam and materials he worked on. "He knew every curve he wanted, going by feeling and what was in his head, and he worked fast. Mask and goggles were a constant. So was loud noise." That was true, whether in Mike's CA workplaces or the now-*ohana* (small rental) located on the Big Island. Mike had worked on boards and, particularly, paddles dinged up by Kawaihae paddlers, until his stroke. Three paddles on a weathered board fence still show the way to the Eaton driveway. The fish-shaped logo marks entries to their house and the ohana, once his workshop and now a rental living quarters.

Down the inside hall near the Eatons' door, I admired a framed Star Wars-like cartoon with "Monster Wave" on it. Mike explained, "That's by Mike Dormer, a well-known artist, who hung around my shop. He was always going to put 'Eaton Alive' on tee shirts." Actually, one of those tees hangs in the Eaton closet. I asked if it was difficult to have folks hanging around when he was working so hard, and he shrugged. "I usually made time. It's good PR."

Mike looked out at the Pacific beyond the sun porch from his hospital bed in his photo-decorated room. We moved him to a wheelchair so his good right eye could track the collage of family and friends. I heard "The one of Big Red with the roaring fire is in Pezman's magazine." Numerous gliders-and-clouds elicited "That was a great, high-performance plane. I did a lot of gliding at Warner Springs, San Diego back country." The sculpted wood endorsed with 'Paddler, Craftsman, Friend, Eaton, Mahalo' was "from 'the skipper of the boat where Marianne and I were married.'" Numerous shirtless surfers filled the walls, along with gleaming hot rods, and 'Eaton' logo amidst signed well wishes.

Asked about the autographed flag on an Eaton surfboard and the Mission Beach picture filled with three dozen of his signature surfboards, he said, "Rachel, the web mistress, said 'Let's have a paddle in honor of Mike. Not a race, but the course he used as a workout.' Sixty people showed up with surfboards, paddle boards, and tees with 'Eaton' on 'em."

He went on recalling pictures of "Marianne and Bay to Breakers runners…likeable guys who were 'fumble and bumble' and would be late for their own funeral…friends who used to go to Baja with us…a friendly blond gal whose husband is related to surfing…neighbors—we always made it a point to be good neighbors and put time to good use. Time only comes once. Use it well or it's gone."

That walk down memory lane was the day that Mike wore his "To the End of the Road" cap. He doffed it and told me it represented Pololu Valley, where the road ends in North Kohala. He quickly told me I should check the Hawi Resource Center for Hawaiian storyteller, Kindy Sproat's book. I agreed, thinking how Mike's life was also a Hawaiian-retiree/storyteller's one-of-a-kind story.

1999 Michael Working on a Board

Surfing for a Cure (Mike, Center) 2007

Mike at Local Beach Sunset

Mike on Surfboard

Pololu

A Design of His Own Resources

Brian Brennan, <u>Rod Action magazine,</u> Vol. 13 No.9, "California Dreamin'" p. 58-63 (centerfold)

<u>Boardroom: Legends of Surfboard Shaping</u>, Scott Bass, Producer, <u>www.boardroomthemovie.com</u>, DVD video

Chris Cobbs, "A New Era of Surfers—But Not Really a New Wave", <u>Los Angeles Times, July 11, 1980, p.1</u>

http://easyreader.hermosawave.net/news2002/storypage.asp?StoryID=20027172&IssuePath=news2005/0901

Interviews with Michael Eaton, 55-3229 Akoni Pule, Hawi, HI 96755

Inverviews with Marianne Eaton, Hawi, HI 96755

<u>Encyclopedia of Surfing,</u> Matt Warshaw, "Michael Eaton", p. 176

<u>Essential Surfing</u>, George Orbelian, 1985, SF, CA

<u>History of Surfing</u>, Nat Young, Palm Beach Press,

<u>Rod Action magazine,</u> Vol. 13 No.9, "California Dreamin'" p. 58-63 (centerfold)

Terry Rodgers, "Ageless Wonder Paddles 32 Miles in 10 Hours", <u>The San Diego Union Tribune</u>, August 28, 2000, p. D13

http://zippifish.wordpress.com/tag/dan-bendickson/

"The Long Run" Interview, <u>Surfer</u>, 29, 9, 9/1988, pp 61-74, 150.

<u>Surfer's Journal</u>, 24.5, Quiksilver-Waterman Collection, October-November 2015